A Technique for Producing Ideas

A Technique for Producing Ideas

James Webb Young

Waking Lion Press

ISBN 978-1-4341-0275-1

Published by Waking Lion Press, an imprint of The Editorium

This book was originally published in 1940, and additional material was added in 1960. Nevertheless, the copyright was never renewed, placing both the book and the additional material into the public domain.

Waking Lion Press™, the Waking Lion Press logo, and The Editorium™ are trademarks of The Editorium, LLC

The Editorium, LLC
West Valley City, UT 84128-3917
wakinglionpress.com
wakinglion@editorium.com

Contents

Foreword

Chairman, Worldwide and Chief Executive Officer,
Doyle Dane Bernbach Inc.

James Webb Young conveys in his little book something more valuable than the most learned and detailed texts on the subject of advertising. For he is talking about the soul of a piece of communications and not merely the flesh and bones. He is talking about the idea. A chemist can inexpensively put together a human body. What he can't do is spark it with life. Mr. Young writes about the creative spark, the ideas, which bring spirit and life to an advertisement. Nothing is more important to the practice of our craft.

Mr. Young is in the tradition of some of our greatest thinkers when he describes the workings of the creative process. It is a tribute to him that such scientific giants as Bertrand Russell and Albert Einstein have written similarly on this subject. They agree that knowledge is basic to good creative thinking but that it is not enough, that this knowledge must be digested and eventually emerge in the form of fresh, new combinations and relationships. Einstein refers to this as intuition, which he considers the only path to new insights.

The quality of the ideas you get cannot be guaranteed and James Webb Young would, I am sure, be the first one to tell you this. That quality would be the result of all the forces in your life that have played on you, including your genes. But you will be making the most of those forces and all your natural equipment if you follow the procedures he outlines so simply and lucidly.

We are indebted to Mr. Young for getting to the heart of the matter. The result of many years of work in advertising have proved to him that the key element in communications success is the production of relevant and dramatic ideas. He not only makes this point vividly for us but shows us the road to that goal.

Prefatory Note

These thoughts were first presented to graduate students in advertising at the School of Business of the University of Chicago, and later before several gatherings of active advertising practitioners. This accounts for the informal tone.

The subject is properly one which belongs to the professional psychologist, which I am not. This treatment of it, therefore, can have value only as an expression of the personal experience of one who has had to earn his living by producing what were alleged to be ideas.

It was first prepared one Sunday afternoon when I had to consider what I should say to a Monday class. No literature on the subject was at the moment available; nor had I any recollection of having seen any. Since then many readers of this book have called my attention to writings on the same subject, from different areas of experience; and there have been published several recent books with something worthwhile to say on this topic. On the last page of this edition I have listed three which I have found stimulating.

JAMES WEBB YOUNG
Rancho de la Canada, Pena Blanca, New Mexico, July 1960

Chapter 1

How It Started

One day in my last year as an advertising agency executive in Chicago I had a telephone call from the western advertising manager of a well-known magazine.

He asked if he could see me immediately on a matter of importance. Shortly thereafter he arrived in my office, somewhat out of breath.

"We are having a meeting today," he said, "of our entire western sales staff. Its purpose is to discuss how we can improve our selling.

"In our discussions we have tried to analyze the selling methods of other successful publications and salesmen. And among these we have been particularly impressed by the success of Mr. Kobler in his selling of the *American Weekly*.

"After studying just why he is so successful we have come to the conclusion that it all rests on just one thing: he doesn't sell space; he sells Ideas.

"And so," he continued, with enthusiasm, "we have decided that that is just what we are going to do. From here on we are not going to sell space at all. Beginning tomorrow morning every single one of us is going to sell *Ideas!*"

I said I thought that was just dandy, but wondered what it was that he wanted to discuss with me.

"Well," he said, somewhat ruefully, "we could see that what we ought to do is to sell ideas, all right. But after that we sort of got stuck.

"What we are not clear about is just how to get ideas.

"So I said maybe you could tell us, and that is what I am here for.

"You have produced a lot of advertising ideas. Just how do you get them? The boys are waiting for me to come back and tell them."

Now I know that if I had not been so flattered by this question, and if my questioner had not been so obviously serious in asking it, I would have had a hearty fit of laughing at this point.

I thought at the time that I had never heard a funnier or more naive question. And I was completely unable to give any helpful answer to it. But it struck me afterward that maybe the question "How do you get ideas?" wasn't as silly as it sounded. Maybe there was some answer to it. And off and on I thought about it.

Chapter 2

The Formula of Experience

An idea, I thought, has some of that mysterious quality which romance lends to tales of the sudden appearance of islands in the South Seas.

There, according to ancient mariners, in spots where the charts showed only deep blue sea—there would suddenly appear a lovely atoll above the surface of the waters. An air of magic hung about it.

And so it is, I thought, with Ideas. They appear just as suddenly above the surface of the mind; and with that same air of magic and unaccountability. But the scientist knows that the South Sea atoll is the work of countless, unseen coral builders, working below the surface of the sea.

And so I asked myself: "Is an idea, too, like this? Is it only the final result of a long series of unseen idea building processes which go on beneath the surface of the conscious mind?

"If so, can these processes be identified, so that they can consciously be followed and utilized? In short, can a formula or technique be developed in answer to the question: How do you get ideas?"

The Formula of Experience

What I now propose to you is the result of a longtime pondering of these questions; and of close observation of the work of idea producing men with whom I have had associations.

This has brought me to the conclusion that the production of ideas is just as definite a process as the production of Fords; that the production of ideas, too, runs on an assembly line; that in this production the mind follows an *operative technique* which can be learned and controlled; and that its effective use is just as much a matter of *practice in the technique* as is the effective use of any tool.

If you ask me why I am willing to give away the valuable formula of this discovery I will confide to you that experience has taught me two things about it:

First, the formula is so simple to state that few who hear it really believe in it.

Second, while simple to state, it actually requires the hardest kind of intellectual work to follow, so that not all who accept it use it.

Thus I broadcast this formula with no real fear of glutting the market in which I make my living.

Chapter 3

The Pareto Theory

Now, we all know men of whom we have said: "He never had an idea in his life."

That saying brings us face to face with the first real question about this subject. Even assuming that there may be a technique for producing ideas, is everybody capable of using it? Or is there, in addition, some special ability for producing ideas which, after all, you must be born with—like a color sense or tone sense, or card sense?

One answer to that question is suggested in the work *Mind and Society,* by the great Italian sociologist, Pareto.

Pareto thought that all the world could be divided into two main types of people. These types he called, in the French in which he wrote, the *speculator* and the *rentier.*

In this classification speculator is a term used somewhat in the sense of our word "speculative." The speculator is the speculative type of person. And the distinguishing characteristic of this type, according to Pareto, is that he is *constantly preoccupied with the possibilities of new combinations.*

Please hold that italicized definition in mind, because we

shall return to it later. Note particularly that word *preoccu-pied,* with its brooding quality.

Pareto includes among the persons of this speculative type not only the business enterprisers—those who deal with financial and business schemes—but those engaged with inventions of every sort, and with what he calls "political and diplomatic reconstructions."

In short, the type includes all those persons in any field who (like our President Roosevelt) can not let well enough alone, and who speculate on how to change it.

The term used by Pareto to describe the other type, the *rentier,* is translated into English as the stockholder—though he sounds more like the bag holder to me. Such people, he says, are the routine, steady-going, unimaginative, conserving people, whom the *speculator* manipulates.

Whatever we may think of the adequacy of this theory of Pareto's as an entire explanation of social groups, I think we all recognize that these two types of human beings do exist. Whether they were born that way, or whether their environment and training made them that way, is beside the point. They *are.*

This being the case I suppose it must be true that there are large numbers of people whom no technique for producing ideas will ever help.

But it seems to me that the important point for our purpose is that the *speculators,* or reconstructors of this world, are a very large group. Theirs at least is the inherent capacity to produce ideas, and it is by no means such a rare capacity. And so, while perhaps not all God's chilluns got wings, enough have for each of us to hope that we may be among those that have. At any rate, I propose to assume that if a man (or woman) is at all fascinated by advertising it is probably because he is among the reconstructors of this world. Therefore he has some creative powers; and these powers, like others, may be increased by making a deliberate effort to do so, and by mastering a technique for their better use.

Chapter 4

Training the Mind

Assuming, then, that we have some natural capacity for the creation of ideas, we come to the practical question: "What are the means of developing it?"

In learning any art the important things to learn are, first, Principles; and second, Method. This is true of the art of producing ideas.

Particular bits of knowledge are nothing, because they are made up of what Dr. Robert Hutchins once called rapidly aging facts. Principles and method are everything. Thus in advertising we may know the names of types, how much engravings cost, what the rates and closing dates are in a thousand publications; we may know enough grammar and rhetoric to confound a schoolteacher; and enough names of television artists to hold our own at a broadcaster's cocktail party: we may know all these things and still not be an advertising man, because we have no understanding of the principles and fundamental methods by which advertising works.

On the other hand, we may know none of these things but have insight into advertising principles and method, so that by employing technicians to help us we may produce advertising results. Thus we sometimes see a manufacturer or merchant who is a better advertising man than his advertising agent or manager. So with the art of producing ideas. What is most valuable to know is not where to look for a particular idea, but how to train the mind in the *method* by which all ideas are produced; and how to grasp the *principles* which are at the source of all ideas.

Chapter 5

Combining Old Elements

With regard to the general principles which underlie the production of ideas, it seems to me that there are two which are important.

The first of these has already been touched upon in the quotation from Pareto: namely, that an idea is nothing more nor less than a *new combination* of old elements.

This is, perhaps, the most important fact in connection with the production of ideas. However, I want to leave the elaboration of it until we come to a discussion of method. Then we can see the importance of this fact more clearly, through the application of it.

The second important principle involved is that the capacity to bring old elements into new combinations depends largely on the ability to see relationships.

Here, I suspect, is where minds differ to the greatest degree when it comes to the production of ideas. To some minds each fact is a separate bit of knowledge. To others it is a link in a chain of knowledge. It has relationships and similarities. It is not so much a fact as it is an illustration of a general law applying to a whole series of facts.

An illustration of this might be taken from a relationship between advertising and psychiatry. At first blush it might be hoped that there is no relationship! But the psychiatrists have discovered the profound influence which words have in the lives of their patients—words as symbols of emotional experiences.

And now Dr. Harold Lasswell has carried over these word symbol studies of the psychiatrists to the field of political action, and shown how word symbols are used with the same emotional force in propaganda.

To a mind which is quick to see relationships several ideas will occur, fruitful for advertising, about this use of words as symbols. Is this, then, why the change of one word in a headline can make as much as 50 percent difference in advertising response? Can words, studied as emotional symbols, yield better advertising education than words studied as parts of rhetoric? What is the one word symbol which will best arouse the emotion with which I wish this particular advertisement to be charged? And so on.

The point is, of course, that when relationships of this kind are seen they lead to the extraction of a general principle. This general principle, when grasped, suggests the key to a new application, a new combination, and the result is an idea.

Consequently the habit of mind which leads to a search for relationships between facts becomes of the highest importance in the production of ideas. Now this habit of mind can undoubtedly be cultivated. I venture to suggest that, for the advertising man, one of the best ways to cultivate it is by study in the social sciences. A book like Veblen's *Theory of the Leisure Class,* or Riesman's *The Lonely Crowd,* therefore becomes a better book about advertising than most books about advertising.

Chapter 6

Ideas Are New Combinations

With these two general principles in mind—the principle that
an idea is a new combination, and the principle that the ability to make new combinations is heightened by an ability to
see relationships—with these in mind let us now look at the
actual method or procedure by which ideas are produced.

As I said before, what I am now about to contend is that
in the production of ideas the mind follows a method which
is just as definite as the method by which, say, Fords are produced.

In other words, that there is a technique for the use of the
mind for this purpose; that whenever an idea is produced this
technique is followed, consciously or unconsciously; and that
this technique can consciously be cultivated, and the ability
of the mind to produce ideas thereby increased.

This technique of the mind follows five steps. I am sure
that you will all recognize them individually. But the important thing is to recognize their relationship, and to grasp the
fact that the mind follows these five steps in definite order—
that by no possibility can one of them be taken before the
preceding one is completed, if an idea is to be produced.

13

The first of these steps is for the mind to gather its raw material.

That, I am sure, will strike you as a simple and obvious truth. Yet it is really amazing to what degree this step is ignored in practice.

Gathering raw material in a real way is not as simple as it sounds. It is such a terrible chore that we are constantly trying to dodge it. The time that ought to be spent in material gathering is spent in wool gathering. Instead of working systematically at the job of gathering raw material we sit around hoping for inspiration to strike us. When we do that we are trying to get the mind to take the fourth step in the idea-producing process while we dodge the preceding steps.

The materials which must be gathered are of two kinds: they are specific and they are general.

In advertising, the specific materials are those relating to the product and the people to whom you propose to sell it. We constantly talk about the importance of having an intimate knowledge of the product and the consumer, but in fact we seldom work at it.

This, I suppose, is because a real knowledge of a product, and of people in relation to it, is not easy to come by. Getting it is something like the process which was recommended to De Maupassant as the way to learn to write. "Go out into the streets of Paris," he was told by an older writer, "and pick out a cab driver. He will look to you very much like every other cab driver. But study him until you can describe him so that he is seen in your description to be an individual, different from every other cab driver in the world."

This is the real meaning of that trite talk about getting an intimate knowledge of a product and its consumers. Most of us stop too soon in the process of getting it. If the surface differences are not striking we assume that there are no differences. But if we go deeply enough, or far enough, we nearly always find that between every product and some consumers there is an *individuality of relationship* which may lead to an idea.

Thus, for example, I could cite you the advertising for a well-known soap. At first there appeared nothing to say about it that had not been said for many soaps.

But a study was made of the relation of soap to skin and hair—a study which resulted in a fair-sized book on the subject. And out of this book came copy ideas for five years of advertising; ideas which multiplied the sales of this soap by ten in that period. This is what is meant by gathering specific materials.

Of equal importance with the gathering of these specific materials is the continuous process of gathering general materials.

Every really good creative person in advertising whom I have ever known has always had two noticeable characteristics. First, there was no subject under the sun in which he could not easily get interested—from, say Egyptian burial customs to Modern Art. Every facet of life had fascination for him. Second, he was an extensive browser in all sorts of fields of information. For it is with the advertising man as with the cow: no browsing, no milk.

Now this gathering of general materials is important because this is where the previously stated principle comes in— namely, that an idea is nothing more nor less than a new combination of elements. In advertising an idea results from a new combination of *specific knowledge* about products and people with *general knowledge* about life and events.

The process is something like that which takes place in the kaleidoscope. The kaleidoscope, as you know, is an instrument which designers sometimes use in searching for new patterns. It has little pieces of colored glass in it, and when these are viewed through a prism they reveal all sorts of geometrical designs. Every turn of its crank shifts these bits of glass into a new relationship and reveals a new pattern. The mathematical possibilities of such new combinations in the kaleidoscope are enormous, and the greater the number of pieces of glass in it the greater become the possibilities for new and striking combinations.

So it is with the production of ideas for advertising—or anything else. The construction of an advertisement is the construction of a new pattern in this kaleidoscopic world in which we live. The more of the elements of that world which are stored away in that patternmaking machine, the mind, the more the chances are increased for the production of new and striking combinations, or ideas. Advertising students who get restless about the "practical" value of general college subjects might consider this.

This, then, is the first step in the technique of producing ideas: the gathering of materials. Part of it, you will see, is a current job and part of it is a lifelong job. Before passing on to the next step there are two practical suggestions I might make about this material-gathering process.

The first is that if you have any sizable job of specific material gathering to do it is useful to learn the card-index method of doing it.

This is simply to get yourself a supply of those little 3x5 ruled white cards, and use them to write down the items of specific information as you gather them. If you do this, one item to a card, after a while you can begin to classify them by sections of your subject. Eventually you will have a whole file box of them, neatly classified.

The advantage of this method is not merely in such things as bringing order into your work, and disclosing gaps in your knowledge. It lies even more in the fact that it keeps you from shirking the material-gathering job; and by forcing your mind to go through the expression of your material in writing really prepares it to perform its idea-producing processes.

The second suggestion is that for storing up certain kinds of general material some method of doing it like a scrapbook or file is useful.

You will remember the famous scrapbooks which appear throughout the Sherlock Holmes stories, and how the master detective spent his spare time indexing and cross-indexing the odd bits of material he gathered there. We run across an enormous amount of fugitive material which can be grist to the idea producer's mill—newspaper clippings, publication articles, and original observations. Out of such material it is possible to build a useful source book of ideas.

Once I jotted in such a book the question: "Why does every man hope his first child will be a boy?" Five years later it became the headline and idea for one of the most successful advertisements I ever produced.

Chapter 7

The Mental Digestive Process

Now, assuming that you have done a workmanlike job of gathering material—that you have really worked at the first step—what is the next part of the process that the mind must go through? It is the process of masticating these materials, as you would food that you are preparing for digestion.

This part of the process is harder to describe in concrete terms because it goes on entirely inside your head.

What you do is to take the different bits of material which you have gathered and feel them all over, as it were, with the tentacles of the mind. You take one fact, turn it this way and that, look at it in different lights, and feel for the meaning of it. You bring two facts together and see how they fit.

What you are seeking now is the relationship, a synthesis where everything will come together in a neat combination, like a jigsaw puzzle.

And here a strange element comes in. This is that facts sometimes yield up their meaning quicker when you do not scan them too directly, too literally. You remember the winged messenger whose wings could only be seen when glanced at obliquely? It is like that. In fact, it is almost like *listening* for the meaning instead of *looking* for it. When creative people are in this stage of the process they get their reputation for absentmindedness.

As you go through this part of the process two things will happen. First, little tentative or partial ideas will come to you. Put these down on paper. Never mind how crazy or incomplete they seem: get them down. These are foreshadowings of the real idea that is to come, and expressing these in words forwards the process. Here again the little 3x5 cards are useful.

The second thing that will happen is that, by and by, you will get very tired of trying to fit your puzzle together. Let me beg of you not to get tired too soon. The mind, too, has a second wind. Go after at least this second layer of mental energy in this process. Keep trying to get one or more partial thoughts onto your little cards.

But after a while you will reach the hopeless stage. Everything is a jumble in your mind, with no clear insight anywhere. When you reach this point, *if you have first really persisted in efforts to fit your puzzle together*, then the second stage in the whole process is completed, and you are ready for the third one.

* * *

In this third stage you make absolutely no effort of a direct nature. You drop the whole subject, and put the problem out of your mind as completely as you can.

It is important to realize that this is just as definite and just as necessary a stage in the process as the two preceding ones. What you have to do at this time, apparently, is to turn

19

the problem over to your unconscious mind, and let it work while you sleep.

There is one thing you can do in this stage which will help both to put the problem out of consciousness and to stimulate the unconscious, creative processes.

You remember how Sherlock Holmes used to stop right in the middle of a case and drag Watson off to a concert? That was a very irritating procedure to the practical and literal-minded Watson. But Conan Doyle was a creator and knew the creative processes.

So when you reach this third stage in the production of an idea, drop the problem completely, and turn to whatever stimulates your imagination and emotions. Listen to music, go to the theatre or movies, read poetry or a detective story. In the first stage you have gathered your food. In the second you have masticated it well. Now the digestive process is on. Let it alone—but stimulate the flow of gastric juices.

Chapter 8

"Constantly Thinking About It"

Now, if you have really done your part in these three stages of the process you will almost surely experience the fourth.

Out of nowhere the Idea will appear.

It will come to you when you are least expecting it—while shaving, or bathing, or most often when you are half awake in the morning. It may waken you in the middle of the night.

Here, for instance, is the way it happens according to Mary Roberts Rinehart. In her story "Miss Pinkerton" she makes this character say:

"And it was while I was folding up that copy of the Eagle and putting it away for later reading that something came into my mind. I have had this happen before; I can puzzle over a thing until I am in a state of utter confusion, give it up, and then suddenly have the answer leap into my mind without any apparent reason." And here again, is the way it happened in the discovery of the halftone printing process, as told by Mr. Ives, the inventor of it:

"While operating my photo stereotype process in Ithaca I studied the problem of halftone process (*first step*), I went to bed one night in a state of brain fag over the problem (*end of second and beginning of third step*) and the instant that I woke in the morning (*end of third step*) saw before me, apparently projected on the ceiling, the completely worked out process and equipment in operation." (*Fourth step.*) This is the way ideas come: after you have stopped straining for them, and have passed through a period of rest and relaxation from the search.

Thus the story about Sir Isaac Newton and his discovery of the law of gravitation is probably not the whole truth. You will remember that when a lady asked the famous scientist how he came to make the discovery he is said to have replied, "By constantly thinking about it."

It was by constantly thinking about it that he made the discovery possible. But I suspect that if we knew the full history of the case we should find that the actual solution came while he was taking a walk in the country.

Chapter 9

The Final Stage

One more stage you have to pass through to complete the idea-producing process: the stage which might be called the cold, grey dawn of the morning after.

In this stage you have to take your little newborn idea out into the world of reality. And when you do you usually find that it is not quite the marvelous child it seemed when you first gave birth to it.

It requires a deal of patient working over to make most ideas fit the exact conditions, or the practical exigencies, under which they must work. And here is where many good ideas are lost. The idea man, like the inventor, is often not patient enough or practical enough to go through with this adapting part of the process. But it has to be done if you are to put ideas to work in a workaday world.

Do not make the mistake of holding your idea close to your chest at this stage. Submit it to the criticism of the judicious.

When you do, a surprising thing will happen. You will find that a good idea has, as it were, self-expanding qualities. It stimulates those who see it to add to it. Thus possibilities in it which you have overlooked will come to light.

* * *

This, then, is the whole process or method by which ideas are produced:

First, the gathering of raw materials—both the materials of your immediate problem and the materials which come from a constant enrichment of your store of general knowledge.

Second, the working over of these materials in your mind.

Third, the incubating stage, where you let something beside the conscious mind do the work of synthesis.

Fourth, the actual birth of the Idea—the "Eureka! I have it!" stage.

And fifth, the final shaping and development of the idea to practical usefulness.

Some After-Thoughts

Let me express my gratification at the number of letters which have come to me from readers of the earlier editions. The most gratifying have come from people who say "It works!"—that they have followed the prescription and gotten results.

Many have been from other creative people, entirely outside advertising—poets, painters, engineers, scientists, and even one writer of legal briefs—who say I have described their own experience. This supporting evidence will, I hope, encourage the beginner.

From my own further experience in advertising, government, and public affairs I find no essential points which I would modify in the idea-producing process. There is one, however, on which I would put greater emphasis. This is as to the store of general materials in the idea producer's reservoir. I beg leave to illustrate this by a personal reference.

Some years ago I established my home in New Mexico, and have been living there most of each year since. As a result I became interested in a whole new range of subjects, including Indian life, our Spanish history, native handicrafts, folkways of primitive people, etc.

Out of this grew some ideas about the possibilities of marketing some of the products of that region, by mail. I started with one of them—hand-woven neckties—wrote some advertisements about them, and copy-tested them. The result was a very tidy and interesting business.

The point is this: not only did the idea for starting the business come out of a general knowledge of the Southwest and its people, but all of the *particular* ideas for individual advertisements came from this source. If I had never gotten interested in Indian lore, Spanish-American history, the Spanish language, the handicraft philosophy, and so on, *for their own sake,* I would have had none of the reservoir of material which I believe made this advertising effective.

I have seen the truth of this principle a thousand times in practice. There are some advertisements you just cannot write until you have lived long enough—until, say, you have lived through certain experiences as a spouse, a parent, a business man, or what not. The cycle of the years does something to fill your reservoir, unless you refuse to live spatially and emotionally.

But you can also enormously expand your experience, vicariously. It was the author of *Sard Harker,* I believe, who had never been to South America, yet wrote a corking good adventure book about it. I am convinced, however, that you gather this vicarious experience best, not when you are boning up on it for an immediate purpose, but when you are pursuing it as an end in itself.

Of course, if you consider that your education was finished when you left college, and wouldn't be caught dead with a copy of, say, one of Jane Austen's novels under your pillow, go no farther. In that case you will probably never know how the landed gentry of nineteenth century England scorned people "in trade," nor have any ideas about why the Hudson River Squire strain in this country does the same. And that just possibly, some day, might keep you from producing a really effective series of "snob appeal" advertisements for the "carriage trade." Of course, this is a disappearing race, so maybe it doesn't matter.

But the principle of constantly expanding your experience, both personally and vicariously, does matter tremendously in any idea-producing job. Make no mistake about that.

Another point to encourage you. No doubt you have seen people who seem to spark ideas—good ideas—right off the "top of their heads," without ever going through all this process which I have described.

Sometimes you have only seen the "Eureka! I have it!" stage take place. But sometimes you have also seen the fruits of long discipline in the practices here advocated. This discipline produces a mind so well stocked, and so quick at discerning relationships, as to be capable of such fast production.

Still another point I might elaborate on a little is about words. We tend to forget that words are, themselves, ideas. They might be called ideas in a state of suspended animation. When the words are mastered the ideas tend to come alive again.

Take the word "semantics," for example. The chances are you will never use it in an advertisement. But if you have it in your vocabulary you will have a number of ideas about the use of words as symbols which will be of very practical value indeed. (If you don't have it in your vocabulary, look up Hayakawa's *Language in Thought and Action.*)

Thus, words being symbols of ideas, we can collect ideas by collecting words. The fellow who said he tried reading the dictionary, but couldn't get the hang of the story, simply missed the point: namely, that it is a collection of short stories.

And, finally, let me suggest a few other books which will expand your understanding of this whole idea-producing process:

The Art of Thought by Graham Wallas. Published by Jonathan Gape, Ltd., London.

Science and Method by H. Poincaré. Translation by F. Maitland. Published by Thos. Nelson & Sons, London.

The Art of Scientific Investigation by W.I.B. Beveridge. A Modern Library paperback edition.

88289153R00024

Made in the USA
Columbia, SC
27 January 2018

Thomas Jefferson

UNA VIDA DE PATRIOTISMO

por Ann-Marie Kishel

ediciones Lerner • Minneapolis

La edición en español fue realizada por un equipo de traductores nativos de español de
translations.com, empresa mundial dedicada a la traducción.

ediciones Lerner
Una división de Lerner Publishing Group
241 First Avenue North
Minneapolis, MN 55401 EUA

Dirección de Internet: www.lernerbooks.com

Las palabras en **negrita** se explican en un glosario en la página 31.

Agradecimientos de fotografías

Las fotografías presentes en este libro se reproducen por cortesía de: © Bettmann/CORBIS,
portada, pág. 22; Biblioteca del Congreso, págs. 4, 11 (LC-USZC4-1583), 14 (LC-USZC4-
9904), 16 (LC-USZ62-1306), 21, 24 (LC-USZC4-3254), 26 (LC-USZ62-816); © North Wind
Picture Archives, págs. 6, 8, 10, 12, 18, 23; Archivos Nacionales, págs. 15, 27 (fotografía núm.
W & C #66); © James Marrinan, pág. 20; Centro de Información de la Biblioteca Pública de
Minneapolis, pág. 25.

Library of Congress Cataloging-in-Publication Data

Kishel, Ann-Marie.
    [Thomas Jefferson. Spanish]
    Thomas Jefferson : una vida de patriotismo / por Ann-Marie Kishel.
        p. cm. – (Libros para avanzar)
    Includes index.
    ISBN-13: 978-0-8225-6238-2 (lib. bdg. : alk. paper)
    ISBN-10: 0-8225-6238-3 (lib. bdg. : alk. paper)
    1. Jefferson, Thomas, 1743–1826–Juvenile literature.
    2. Presidents–United States–Juvenile literature. I. Title. II. Series.
    E332.79.K5718 2007
    973.4'6–dc22   2006006698

Contenido

Thomas Jefferson

Una vida de patriotismo

Thomas Jefferson fue el tercer
presidente de los Estados Unidos
de América. También redactó la
Declaración de la Independencia.
Thomas amaba a los Estados Unidos.
Hizo muchas cosas para demostrar
su **patriotismo**.

Es posible que la escuela a la que asistió Thomas se pareciera a esta.

Primeros años

Cuando era niño, a Thomas le encantaban los libros. Sabía que tenía que aprender. Trabajaba duro en las tareas de la escuela. Tenía un cuaderno donde escribía sobre las cosas que veía y escuchaba. Cuando era joven, a veces se pasaba 15 horas por día estudiando.

Thomas trabajó en el capitolio colonial, en Williamsburg, Virginia.

La democracia

Cuando Thomas creció, lo eligieron para ayudar a gobernar Virginia. Virginia era una **colonia** británica. El rey de Gran Bretaña gobernaba a las colonias británicas en Norteamérica. Su gobierno creaba las leyes.

Jorge III era el rey de Gran Bretaña en esa época.

El rey Jorge hacía que los **colonos** pagaran **impuestos** a Gran Bretaña. Los colonos no podían opinar sobre esas leyes. Pensaban que no era justo.

Thomas creía en la **democracia**. Pensaba que la gente debería elegir a sus líderes. Opinaba que la gente debía hacer sus propias leyes.

Las personas estaban enojadas por las leyes del rey.

Soldados coloniales y británicos pelearon en 1776.

La Declaración de la Independencia

Los colonos querían liberarse del rey. Querían crear sus propias leyes. Comenzó una guerra entre los colonos y Gran Bretaña. Se llamó la **Guerra de Independencia**.

Líderes coloniales observan la Declaración de la Independencia.

Thomas ayudó a escribir una carta al rey. Se llamó la Declaración de la Independencia.

Explicaba por qué los colonos debían tener su propio país. La carta enfadó al rey. Quería que las colonias siguieran siendo parte de Gran Bretaña.

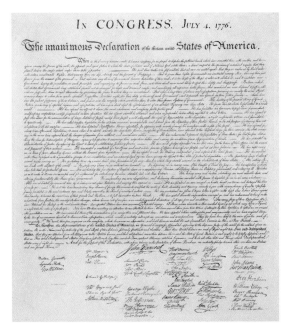

La Declaración de la Independencia se firmó el 4 de julio de 1776.

Copyright,1876 by Currier & Ives N.Y.
GEN.^l HENRY KNOX, Secy. of War.
GEORGE WASHINGTON.
ALEXANDER HAMILTON. Secy. of the Treasury.
THOMAS JEFFERSON. Secy. of State.
EDMUND RANDOLPH, Attorney General.

Estos primeros líderes estadounidenses formaron el primer gobierno.

Un nuevo país

Finalmente, la guerra terminó. Las colonias se convirtieron en un país independiente. Las colonias se convirtieron en un país independente llamado los Estados Unidos. El presidente George Washington le pidió ayuda a Thomas para gobernar el país. Después, John Adams fue elegido presidente. Thomas fue el vicepresidente. Quería ayudar a su país.

Thomas fue a caballo a la ceremonia en que lo nombraron presidente.

Presidente Jefferson

Thomas no estaba contento con la manera en que el presidente Adams gobernaba los Estados Unidos. Pensaba que más personas deberían ayudar a tomar decisiones para el país. Se postuló como candidato para presidente y ganó.

Cuando Thomas fue presidente, los Estados Unidos tenían **deudas**. Thomas se aseguró de que el gobierno gastara menos dinero.

Cuando Thomas fue presidente, el dinero tenía este aspecto.

El secretario del Tesoro, Albert Gallatin, ayudó a Thomas a reducir la deuda.

También encontró maneras para que el país ganara más dinero. El dinero extra se usó para pagar la mitad de las deudas del país.

Thomas Jefferson firma la Compra de Luisiana.

Mientras Thomas fue presidente, los Estados Unidos compraron un gran territorio a Francia. Esto se llamó la **Compra de Luisiana**.

Este territorio estaba entre el río
Mississippi y las montañas Rocosas.
Con él, los Estados Unidos se hicieron
mucho más grandes.

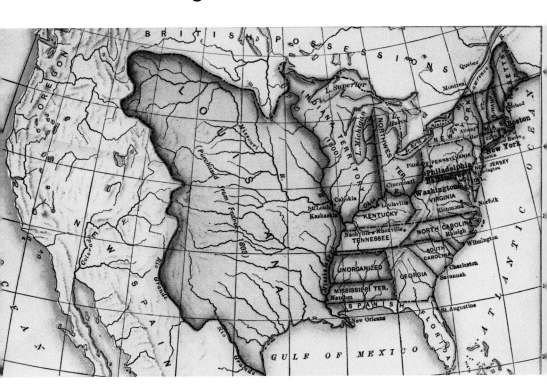

Thomas fue presidente durante ocho años. Sentía que había sido presidente el tiempo suficiente.

La casa de Thomas en Virginia se llama Monticello.

Pensaba que era hora de que los Estados Unidos tuvieran un nuevo presidente. Thomas volvió a su casa.

Thomas Jefferson demostró su patriotismo ayudando a su país.

Esta familia demuestra su patriotismo celebrando el Día de la Independencia.

Trabajó duro para hacer de los Estados
Unidos un lugar mejor. Sus decisiones
ayudaron a su país y a su gente.

CRONOLOGÍA DE THOMAS JEFFERSON

1743
Thomas Jefferson nace el 13 de abril.

1779
Es elegido gobernador de Virginia.

1776
Redacta la Declaración de la Independencia.

1790
Se convierte en el primer secretario de estado de los Estados Unidos.

1797
Se convierte en vicepresidente del gobierno del presidente John Adams.

1819
Crea la Universidad de Virginia.

1801
Se convierte en el tercer presidente de los Estados Unidos.

1826
Thomas Jefferson muere el 4 de julio.

Más sobre Thomas Jefferson

● Thomas Jefferson quería ser recordado como el autor de la Declaración de la Independencia y como el padre de la Universidad de Virginia.

● El rostro de Thomas Jefferson aparece en las monedas de cinco centavos y los billetes de dos dólares.

● Justo antes de que Thomas Jefferson fuera presidente, la Casa Blanca pasó de Filadelfia, Pensilvania, a Washington, D.C.

Sitios Web

Biography of Thomas Jefferson
http://www.whitehouse.gov/history/presidents/tj3.html

Monticello: The Home of Thomas Jefferson
http://www.monticello.org/

Thomas Jefferson
http://www.americaslibrary.gov/cgi-bin/page.cgi/aa/jefferson

Glosario

colonia: territorio gobernado por otro país

colono: persona que vive en una colonia

Compra de Luisiana: compra de un gran territorio que Francia vendió a los Estados Unidos

Declaración de la Independencia: carta que explica por qué Gran Bretaña no debería gobernar a las colonias Norteamericanas

democracia: gobierno en el cual las personas eligen a sus líderes y ayudan a hacer las leyes

deuda: dinero que una persona o país debe a otro

Guerra de Independencia: guerra entre Gran Bretaña y las colonias británicas en Norteamérica desde 1775 hasta 1783

impuestos: dinero que una persona paga a un gobierno

patriotismo: amor de una persona por su país

Índice